A BLUE BANNER BIOGRAPHY

Queen Latifah

By Kathleen Tracy

Mitchell Lane
PUBLISHERS

P.O. Box 196
Hockessin, Delaware 19707
Visit us on the web: www.mitchelllane.com
Comments? email us: mitchelllane@mitchelllane.com

Mitchell Lane
PUBLISHERS

Printing   2   3   4   5   6   7   8   9

Blue Banner Biographies

Avril Lavigne	Beyoncé	Bow Wow
Clay Aiken	Daniel Radcliffe	Eminem
Eve	Ja Rule	Jay Z
Jodie Foster	Mary-Kate and Ashley Olsen	Melissa Gilbert
Michael Jackson	Missy Elliott	Nelly
P. Diddy	**Queen Latifah**	Richie Valens
Rita Williams-Garcia	Ron Howard	Rudy Giuliani
Sally Field	Shirley Temple	

Library of Congress Cataloging-in-Publication Data
Tracy, Kathleen
         Queen Latifah / by Kathleen Tracy
                    p. cm. – (A blue banner biography.)
Includes bibliographical references (p.), discography (p.), and index.
         ISBN 1-58415-313-X (library bound)
         1. Latifah, Queen – Juvenile literature. 2. Rap Musicians – United States – Biography – Juvenile
         literature. I. Title. II. Series.

ML3930.L178T73 2004
782.421649′092–dc22
                                                                                                                    2004009174

ABOUT THE AUTHOR: Kathleen Tracy has been a journalist for over twenty years. Her writing has been featured in magazines including The Toronto Star's "Star Week", *A&E Biography* magazine, *KidScreen* and *TV Times*. She is also the author of numerous biographies including "The Boy Who Would be King" (Dutton), "Jerry Seinfeld" - The Entire Domain" (Carol Publishing), "Don Imus - America's Cowboy" (Carroll & Graf), "Mariano Guadalupe Vallejo," and "William Hewlett: Pioneer of the Computer Age," both for Mitchell Lane. She recently completed "God's Will?" for Sourcebooks.

PHOTO CREDITS: Cover: Gregg DeGuire/WireImage.com; p. 4 Kevin Winter/Getty Images; p. 10 Dan Steinberg/Getty Images; p. 16 Barry King/WireImage.com; p. 25 Chris Pizzello/Associated Press; p. 29 Gregg DeGuire/WireImage.com.

ACKNOWLEDGMENTS: The following story has been thoroughly researched, and to the best of our knowledge, represents a true story. While every possible effort has been made to ensure accuracy, the publisher will not assume liability for damages caused by inaccuracies in the data, and makes no warranty on the accuracy of the information contained herein. This story has not been authorized nor endorsed by Queen Latifah.

CONTENTS

Chapter 1
Down the Red Carpet... 5

Chapter 2
A New Jersey Tomboy.. 9

Chapter 3
Music Royalty 14

Chapter 4
Overcoming Personal Loss 19

Chapter 5
An All-Around Performer 24

Chronology 29

Filmography... 30

Discography 31

For Further Reading 32

Index 32

Although she started her career as a rap artist, Queen Latifah has become one of Hollywood's most popular and glamorous movie stars. Here she poses for photographers on the red carpet at the 75th Annual Academy Awards in March 2003.

Down the Red Carpet

*T*he Academy Award telecast is the Super Bowl of the film industry. Seen by almost one billion people in over 100 countries around the globe, it is the most watched event of its kind. When the actors, writers, musicians, executives, and technicians who were nominated for an Oscar arrived at the theater on a warm afternoon in March, 2003 and stepped out onto the red carpet, most were living out dreams come true. Many could still not quite believe their good fortune. None of them was more surprised to be there than Queen Latifah. She had been nominated for Best Supporting Actress.

The United States had recently declared war on Iraq. So the traditional televised walk down the red carpet in front of hundreds of photographers and journalists from all over the world had been cut back to a short stroll into Hollywood's Kodak Theatre with only a few photographers on hand. Even though the media hoopla was toned down outside the theater, inside there was still excitement in the air as the nominees arrived. Queen Latifah posed for photographers in an elegant blue evening gown.

She described to Wilson Morales of blackfilm.com what it felt like to get the phone call telling her she had been nominated for an Oscar. "It's pretty intense. It's pretty high. You just take off. I wasn't expecting that call."

She had just come home from spending the weekend at the NBA All-Star basketball game.

"I just went jumping and running around the house," Latifah said about the Oscar nomination.

"I was up all night watching the first season of *Good Times* on the tour bus on the way back home," she continued. "It was very drafty on the bus and I couldn't sleep. I was drowsy when I got home, and just got under my covers when the phone rang. It was my partner Shakim Compere, and he was like *Yo, we got the nomination!* and I was like *What nomination?* He said, *The Oscar nomination*, and I was like *No way*. So I just went jumping and running around the house and screaming and woke up my best friend. My assistant was downstairs sleeping and I dived on top of her and woke her up. I said *Yo, we got it!* It was pretty exhilarating. I was shocked."

Some of her fans may have been shocked that the nomination wasn't for having written a song that appeared in a film. Rather, it was for her performance in the musical *Chicago*. She played the role of a sassy jail guard named Mama Morton. Not only was she the only African American to be nominated for an Academy Award in 2003, she also made history as the first hip-hop artist ever to be contending for an Oscar.

It was the 75th anniversary of the Academy Awards. "They're getting hip in their old age," Latifah happily commented in an interview with the *Toronto Sun*. "They're getting kind of sharp there."

Latifah was more than a spectator at the ceremony. She performed a duet with her *Chicago* co-star, Catherine Zeta-Jones. They sang "I Move On," one of five nominees for Best Song. Latifah replaced Renee Zelwegger, who sang the song with Zeta-Jones in the movie. Zelwegger did not have much musical experience. She admitted she would be too nervous to sing live in front of so many people. The

> *Latifah made history as the first hip-hop artist ever to be contending for an Oscar.*

show's producers knew that Latifah had absolutely no problem performing and asked her to take Renee's place.

Though *Chicago* won the Academy Award for Best Picture of the year, Latifah didn't win the Oscar for Best Supporting Actress. It went to Zeta-Jones. Yet Latifah knew that being nominated for an Oscar and performing in the ceremonies was a personal and professional turning point. She was still an icon for hip-hop fans the world over. Now she had also crossed over and won a large mainstream audience who knew her primarily as an actress.

> **Her Oscar nomination and performing in the ceremonies was a turning point for Latifah.**

Success seldom comes easily. For Latifah, it had been a long, sometimes painful, struggle. Perhaps her biggest accomplishment was that despite all she had achieved, she had never compromised herself. In the process, she became a role model for young people everywhere.

A New Jersey Tomboy

*L*ong before she became known as Queen Latifah to her fans, she was Dana Elaine Owens. Born March 18, 1970 in Newark, New Jersey, Dana grew up in an industrial area that had more smokestacks than trees. Her dad, Lance, was a policeman who spent hours teaching Dana karate, gun handling and how to camp, skills he had learned while in the army.

"I'm not afraid of too many things," Latifah would later tell *People* magazine, "and I got that invincible kind of attitude from him."

Growing up, young Dana was a tomboy and a self-described handful, always rambunctious and full of energy.

"Give her a pot, she'd bang it," Rita Owens, her mom, told *People*. "A spoon, she'd sing into it. A box, she'd beat it."

Looking back now, Latifah understands that emotional issues from his service in the Vietnam War plagued her dad. These issues ultimately caused her parents to divorce when she was eight years old.

After the split, Dana moved with her mom and older brother, Lance, Jr., into an East Newark housing project. Rita was determined to give her children a better life. She worked two jobs while attending college, where she earned a teaching degree. After taking a job as an art

As a child, Latifah was very close to her father who taught her martial arts and often took her on camping trips. Even though her parents divorced, they both supported their daughters' dream to be a singer. Above, proud parents Lance and Rita Owens attended Latifah's surprise birthday party in 2003.

teacher at Irvington High School, Rita was able to move her family out of the projects and into a modest home in Newark. Despite the divorce, Dana retained a close relationship with her father.

When Dana was in the second grade, testing had determined that she was "intellectually gifted." Wanting her daughter to have every educational opportunity possible, Rita scrimped and saved so she could send Dana to Saint Anne's parochial school. Not only did Dana excel as a student, she also had a chance to show off her performing talent. When she was in the seventh grade, she starred as Dorothy in the school's production of *The Wiz*.

Music and old Hollywood musicals became increasingly important to Dana as she grew up, especially after one particular conversation she had with her mom. Rita warned her that life would not be easy for an African-American woman in America.

> When Dana was in the second grade, testing had determined she was "intellectually gifted."

"Once you start getting worldly enough, your mind develops enough for you to understand when your mother has that conversation about you being black," Latifah told writer David Germain. "Being black meant that you're going to have to work twice as hard. And you're a female, so you're going to have to work twice as hard. And there will be people who will come against you just on those two reasons, those two facts.

"That's a crushing thing to tell a kid. To introduce your child to the fact that you live in a world of racism is tough. So things like musicals were places you could escape to."

> Dana gave herself a Muslim name. "Latifah" means "delicate" or "sensitive" in Arabic.

But at the same time, she told *Edmonton Sun* writer Neal Watson, "I was never taught to fear. I was trusted to a point to find my way in life. Even if I fell a little, that was OK. I had that freedom."

That freedom even allowed her to change her name. When she was eight, Dana decided to give herself a Muslim-sounding name after her brother started calling himself "Jameel." Her Muslim cousin Sharonda suggested "Latifah," which means "delicate" or "sensitive" in Arabic.

"I didn't change my name because I didn't like what my parents had given me," Latifah explained to Jae-Ha Kim of the *Chicago Sun-Times*. "But I knew that picking my own name would be a way of defining myself. And that was important to me even when I was very young."

At Irvington High School, Dana's good nature and sense of humor made her a popular student. She was also athletic and played power forward on the school's state championship basketball team.

"Any sport, I could play," she told the *Toronto Sun*. "I was always acting in the school plays. There was always like five different things going on in my life at the same time since I was in grade school."

For a long time, Latifah wasn't sure what she wanted to do with her life. She considered a variety of careers, from marine biologist to acting.

"You wish for these things when you're a kid, but you never really think it will all come true," she observed to journalist Helen Eisenbach. "But I would watch TV and imitate all the accents: English, Jamaican, Spanish."

It would soon become apparent that Latifah's true passion was music.

Her good nature, sense of humor, and athletic abilities made Dana a popular student.

Music Royalty

*I*n high school, one of Latifah's favorite pastimes was listening to rap music. She and her close friend Shakim Compere, who would later become her business partner, would go hang out in the basement of a local deejay named Mark James and listen to his rap records.

During her sophomore year in high school she joined a female rap group called Ladies Fresh, a move that was fully encouraged and supported by her mother. Even though it was still for the love of the music, Latifah also believed music was a way to make honest money.

"I just loved the music," she told writer Aldore Collier in *Ebony* magazine. "My friends inspired me to get into it. None of us was making any money. We were broke kids but we had a lot of big dreams. We all wanted the Benzes, BMWs, to wear the Guccis and Louis Vuitton.

Rap was how we wanted to make our money instead of being drug dealers."

When she was 16, she made her first record demo.

"It was still a hobby then," she told Collier. "My dream was just to get the record played. They were playing other stuff that we thought was garbage."

The demo flopped but Latifah was not discouraged. A couple of years later, James, who would go on to become a well-known music producer under the name Mark the 45 King, helped pay for another demo of Latifah rapping "Princess of the Posse." Through his music industry contacts, James sent the demo to several labels.

Meanwhile, Latifah was working cleaning tables at Burger King and preparing to attend Borough of Manhattan Community College. She planned to major in broadcast journalism. Then James called and told her an executive at Tommy Boy records had heard the demo and wanted to sign her to a contract. Even though she was thrilled, she refused to change her educational plans.

When Tommy Boy records offered Latifah a contract she refused to change her educational plans.

At the time, almost all rappers were men who added "M.C." in front of their names. As she prepared to record her first single, Latifah wanted to come up with a more distinctive moniker. It didn't take long. "Everybody was M.C. this, M.C. that, and I didn't want to be known as M.C. Latifah," she explained to David Germain. "I had kind of been kicking around 'Queen' because I thought all women should carry themselves as queens, and if they felt that way about themselves they wouldn't go for half the things they do. They wouldn't allow people to just

After she signed her first record deal, Latifah added "Queen" to her name. She liked the name because she feels women should carry themselves like queens. Women should respect themselves and demand respect from others.

treat them any kind of way. And they would feel prideful, respected. So I was like, yeah, queen. That sounds good."

"My mother was like, *Queen? You're 17. I'm the queen.* But she trusted me, and I stuck with it, and it worked."

Even though female rappers were so rare as to be an oddity, Latifah was undeterred.

"I didn't really think about it being almost all men doing rap," she told the *Chicago Sun-Times.* "All I thought about was doing my own thing and making my own album. It didn't really faze me that there weren't a lot of women in the business, or that the women that were around didn't look like me."

Tall at 5'9" and athletic in build, Latifah didn't look like most female singers or rappers and refused to try.

Even though female rappers were rare, Latifah was undeterred.

"There was no way I was going to wear spandex to fit into what everyone else looked like," she continued. "I didn't see the point in that—just like I didn't want to sound like everyone else."

In 1988, she released two singles, "Wrath of My Madness" and "Dance for Me." The success of the records forced Latifah to put her college education on hold. In

1989, she toured Europe and also performed at the famed Apollo Theater in Harlem. On stage, Latifah was an imposing presence, wearing traditional African garments including some elaborate headpieces. That same year she released her first album, *All Hail the Queen*. It went on to sell one million copies and earned Latifah the Best New Artist Award for 1990 by the New Music Seminar of Manhattan.

> **"Ladies First" paid tribute to the contributions black women made in the fight for freedom.**

The second single from *All Hail the Queen*, "Ladies First," paid tribute to the contributions made by black women all over the world in the fight for freedom. The song became a rap classic and was later named one of the "500 Songs That Shaped Rock 'n' Roll" by the Rock and Roll Hall of Fame.

Two more albums followed. By the early 1990s, barely into her 20s, Queen Latifah had become one of music's most important artists.

"I was never sure how it would all be played out," she said in her *Chicago Sun-Times* interview. "But my mother always knew that things would work out well for me. She always knew."

What nobody could have known was that a family tragedy was about to shatter Latifah's world.

Overcoming Personal Loss

While Latifah was building her music career, her brother Lance had followed in their father's footsteps and become a policeman. For his 23rd birthday, Latifah surprised her brother with a brand new motorcycle. Lance and Latifah, who owned two cycles of her own, would go on rides together as often as they could. They enjoyed the feeling of freedom and having the chance to spend some time together.

"We were a tight family," Latifah recalled in an *Ebony* interview. "I didn't fight with my brother growing up. There was a lot of love in my house. We rode those bikes together. For a minute, me and my brother were true best friends."

That all ended in 1992 when Lance was killed after crashing into a car while making a turn on his motorcycle. Latifah had just been riding with her brother three days before the accident.

The loss left a terrible void in Latifah's life. In an effort to deal with her grief, she began playing basketball for hours by herself until she couldn't run anymore. She also briefly turned to drugs and started smoking marijuana. Even though it helped her cope with her feelings of helplessness, she knew it was a wrong choice.

> *Latifah found that her music was the best therapy for dealing with the loss of her brother.*

She didn't take long to stop using drugs. She found that her music was the best therapy. She turned all her energy into working on a new album, *Black Reign*. It reflected the pain Latifah felt at losing her brother. She wrote the song, "Winki's Theme," in his honor. Winki was her brother's nickname. His mother gave it to him because he blinked a great deal as a baby.

"*Black Reign* is about the past year of my life, the hardest year I've ever lived through," she told Deborah Gregory in *Essence* magazine not long after the album came out. "I still can't believe that my brother, my brother is really gone. One stupid turn on a motorcycle and, wham, it's all over. I don't think I'll ever really understand why it happened or why it had to be him. What has got me through this is my relationship with my mom. We've always been so tight, more like sisters really."

Rita urged Latifah to find a positive way to deal with the family's tragedy. The two of them established the Lance Owens Scholarship Foundation. To raise money, they do fundraisers and have an annual banquet. That allows the Foundation to award four scholarships every

Her brothers' death in a motorcycle accident sent Latifah into a deep depression. Eventually, she learned to cope with the loss through her music. In his honor, Latifah and her mom established the Lance Owens Scholarship Foundation.

year. There is one stipulation. The scholarship winners have to return and give back to the community.

In the end, the tragedy reminded her not to take anything for granted. "His death changed my whole perspective on life," she admitted to writer Aldore Collier. "It made me want to live more."

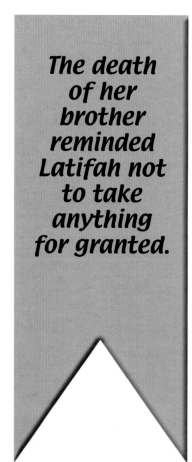

The death of her brother reminded Latifah not to take anything for granted.

The loss of her brother also made Latifah value her friends that much more. Even though she was now a successful performer, she still had the same friends. Many of them were struggling to get their big break. Generous by nature and possessing a savvy business sense, Latifah figured out a way to both help her friends and be profitable at it.

The biggest problem many new artists have is that they are naïve when it comes to the business of music. "Many of us are so uneducated in business matters that we're constantly getting duped while filling the pockets of record companies," Latifah told Deborah Gregory.

In addition to directing her own career, Latifah used her clout as a platinum selling rapper to start a record label and management company. It would look after the careers of the same performers with whom she used to listen to rap records in Mark James's basement.

She called the company Flavor Unit Management. Among the first groups she signed and mentored was Naughty by Nature. The group's two platinum singles, "OPP" and "Hip Hop Hooray" made Flavor Unit one of the top rap labels and management companies in the country — and made Latifah a well-respected record executive as well as performer.

All these achievements in the music industry would have been enough for most people. Not Queen Latifah. She had never given up her dream to be an actress. She set out to become the first rap artist to become a TV and movie star.

Latifah set out to become the first rap artist to become a TV and movie star.

An All-Around
Performer

*E*ven as her first album was on its way to selling a million copies, Latifah had started going on acting auditions. After a few small film roles, Latifah got her big break in 1993 when she was cast in the FOX Network sitcom, *Living Single*. It was about four young professional women trying to make it in New York City. In the series, which co-starred Kim Fields, Kim Coles and Erika Alexander, Latifah played Khadijah James, who runs a magazine.

When she wasn't shooting the series, Latifah—who actually prefers to be called Dana by her friends and family – was busy working on her next album and running Flavor Unit. In 1994 she won a Grammy Award for Best Solo Rap Performance for the song "U.N.I.T.Y.," which denounced violence against women. In addition, Latifah supported several causes, including anti-drug campaigns. In 1997 she was awarded the Aretha Franklin

Award for Entertainer of the Year at the Soul Train Lady of Soul Awards.

The *Living Single* series lasted five years and acted as a springboard for feature film roles. Latifah showed off her dramatic talents in the movie *Set it Off*, playing a bank robber. In the film *Living Out Loud*, many fans were surprised to hear her sing classic ballads like "Lush Life," proving that her singing skills went far beyond rap. After signing a book deal to write her autobiography, Latifah

Already an award-winning recording artist and well-respected record executive, Latifah was determined to become a successful actress as well. She got her first break on the television series "Living Single," and went on to become a popular film actress in movies like "Bringing Down the House."

starred in her own talk show for two years. That introduced her to an even wider audience.

"I feel God blessed me with a lot of talent in different ways," Latifah observed in a *Toronto Sun* interview. "I've always been pretty versatile in my life. I've always done a lot of different things, whether playing basketball, rapping, hanging out, dancing, whatever. She added, "I wanted to be so many things. I never knew that the things I wished for as a child would come true today, but they have."

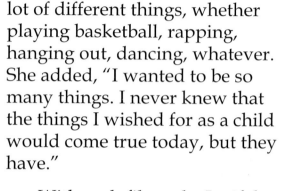

Latifah proved herself to be a performer who appealed to people of all colors and all ages.

With each film role, Latifah further proved herself to be a performer who appealed to people of all colors and all ages. After her standout performance in *Chicago*, Latifah starred in the comedy *Bringing Down the House* opposite Steve Martin. She played a prison inmate who broke out to be with a friend she made via the Internet. The movie made over $100 million and firmly established Latifah as a movie star.

Although she is sometimes overwhelmed at her success, she told Bruce Kirkland of the *Toronto Sun* that she's not really surprised. "I worked for it," she said. "But I'm thankful and I feel blessed. You know, God really looked out for me."

In turn, Latifah feels the need to give back. As she explained to Kirkland, "I'm trying to think of ways that I can apply myself. I want to open up a school for young

Despite her success as a movie star, Latifah remains close to the friends she grew up with. Latifah believes it's important for people to give back to their communities so that young people will have the same opportunities she did.

black males because I feel that they need it the most. Not that the little girls don't, but I feel that, in my community, the brothers need it more than anyone else because they're the men and they have to be the leaders in our community, in our futures."

She would also like to improve the area where she grew up.

"There are so many buildings around here that are just waiting to be renovated and lived in," she said in an *Essence* interview. "My dream is to own beautiful low-income housing that looks like townhouses and not projects, so people can take pride in them. I'd also like to open a chain of Laundromats. Everybody in the 'hood has to wash their clothes, and there is nothing like a nice, clean Laundromat!"

More than anything, Latifah wants to give people a chance to fulfill their potential.

More than anything, Latifah wants to give people a chance to fulfill their potential.

"Everybody on welfare is not trying to rip off the system," she told *Ebony* magazine. "Some are using it as a stepping-stone. In my heart, I want to provide the next step for them. But at the same time, it's up to each of us to make the most of our opportunities. I take everything I get as a blessing. I say my prayers every night, and if it's meant to be, it will be."

1970	Born on March 18 in Newark, New Jersey
1978	Takes name of Latifah; parents are divorced
1988	Signs with Tommy Boy label
1989	Releases her first album, *All Hail the Queen*
1990	Named Best New Artist by the New Music Seminar of Manhattan
1991	Signs with legendary record label Motown
1992	Brother dies in a motorcycle accident
1993	Wins first Grammy
1993	Stars in sitcom *Living Single*
1997	Named entertainer of the year at the Soul Train Awards
1998	Named one of the "Most Fascinating Women of 1998" by *Ladies' Home Journal*
1999	Nominated for two NAACP Image Awards for Outstanding Supporting Actress in a Motion Picture (*Living Out Loud*) and Outstanding Actress in a Television Movie/Mini-Series/Dramatic Special (*Mama Flora's Family*)
1999	Listed as #72 by VH1 on its "100 Greatest Women of Rock & Roll" countdown
1999	Publishes autobiography *Ladies First: Revelations of a Strong Woman*
2003	Nominated for a Golden Globe Award and Academy Award as Best Supporting actress for *Chicago*; wins SAG award as part of Best Ensemble Cast Performance for *Chicago*
2004	Stars in movies *Just Wright* and *Taxi*

FILMOGRAPHY

1991	*House Party 2*
1991	*Jungle Fever*
1992	*Juice*
1993	*My Life*
1993	*Living Single* (TV series)
1996	*Set It Off*
1997	*Hoodlum*
1998	*Sphere*
1998	*Living Out Loud*
1998	*Mama Flora's Family* (TV)
1999	*The Bone Collector*
1999	*Bringing Out the Dead* (voice)
1999	*The Queen Latifah Show* (TV talk show)
2002	*Living with the Dead* (TV miniseries)
2002	*Through the Years of Hip Hop - Vol. 1: Graffiti*
2002	*The Country Bears*
2002	*Pinocchio* (voice)
2002	*Brown Sugar*
2002	*Chicago*
2002	*The O.Z.* (TV)
2003	*Will & Grace* (guest spot)
2003	*Bringing Down the House*
2003	*Scary Movie 3*
2004	*Barbershop 2: Back in Business*
2004	*The Cookout*

DISCOGRAPHY

1989 *All Hail The Queen* (Tommy Boy)
1991 *Nature Of A Sista* (Tommy Boy)
1991 *Latifah's Had It Up 2 Here* (Tommy Boy)
1993 *U.N.I.T.Y.* (Motown)
1993 *Black Reign* (Motown)
1994 *Black Hand Side* (Motown)
1994 *Rough* (Motown)
1994 *Just Another Day* (Motown)
1997 *It's Alright* (Tommy Boy)
1998 *Queen Latifah & The Original Flava Unit* (Old School)
1998 *How Do I Love Thee* (Tommy Boy)
1998 *Order In The Court* (Motown)
2002 *She's A Queen: A Collection Of Hits* (Motown)
2002 *Go Head & She's A Queen* (Motown)
2003 *Better Than the Rest* (Hollywood Records)

FOR FURTHER READING

Bloom, Sarah R. *Queen Latifah* (Black Americans of Achievement). Broomall, Pennsylvania: Chelsea House Publishing, 2001.

Queen Latifah. *Ladies First: Revelations of a Strong Woman*. New York: William Morrow, 1999.

Ruth, Amy. *Queen Latifah*. Minneapolis, Minnesota: Lerner, 2000.

Williams, Terrie. Introduction by Queen Latifah. *Stay Strong: Simple Life Lessons for Teens*. New York: Scholastic, 2002.

INDEX

Academy Awards   5

Chicago   *7-8*

Compere, Shakim   14

Lance Owens Scholarship
Foundation   21

Living Single   24

Queen Latifa
Adding "Queen"   16-17
Brothers' death   19

Changing name to
Latifah   12

Childhood   9

Education   11

Goals   27-28

Ladies Fresh   14

Oscar nomination   6